# Aro
# Os._ _ ᴜᴜ

# Richard Bell

WILLOW
ISLAND
EDITIONS

ALSO BY RICHARD BELL

*Around Old Horbury*

*Waterton's Park*

*Thornes Park*

*Coxley Valley*

*Sandal Castle*

*Malham Magic*

*Village Walks in West Yorkshire*
(Countryside Books)

*Yorkshire Rock*
(British Geological Survey)


© Richard Bell 2002
Published by Willow Island Editions,
41 Water Lane, Middlestown,
Wakefield, WF4 4PX

First published 1998
Second edition 2002

www.willowisland.co.uk


ISBN 1 902467-01-9

# CONTENTS

**Map**      *4*

1. Town Hall      *9*

2. Ossett Market      *10*

3. Library      *12*

4. Yorkshire Bank      *13*

5. Temperance Hall      *14*

6. Barclay's Bank      *15*

7. Pinfold      *17*

8. Mount Zion      *18*

9. Holy Trinity      *20*

10. Christ Church      *22*

11. Brockson Carpets      *24*

12. Park House      *26*

13. Goring House      *28*

14. Tram depot      *29*

15. Gawthorpe Water Tower      *30*

16. Low Laithes      *32*

**Timeline**      *34*

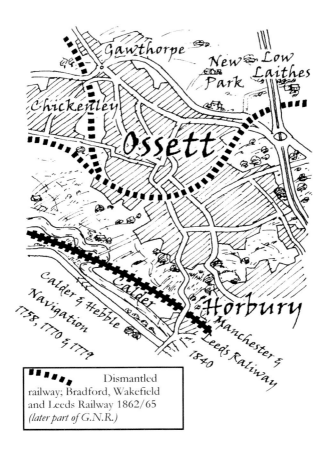

Gawthorpe

New Low
Park Laithes

Chickenley

Ossett

Calder & Hebble
Navigation
1758, 1770 & 1779

Calder

Horbury

Manchester &
Leeds Railway
1840

Dismantled
railway; Bradford, Wakefield
and Leeds Railway 1862/65
*(later part of G.N.R.)*

THE NAME **OSSETT** is Viking and may mean either *'Osla's seat'* or *'ridge camp'*. A ridge isn't as easily defended as an isolated hill-top site, like that of Horbury, which was an earlier Anglo-Saxon settlement *('fortified place in the mud')*. When the Vikings arrived from about 900 A.D. onwards they found the better sites had already been settled by the Anglo-Saxons. The original Celtic people, referred to as Welsh or Britons by the later settlers, still farmed at *Wal*ton and *Bret*ton.

The name of the **Calder** goes back to Celtic times. It means *'spring or hard water'*.

**Streetside** was the name the Anglo-Saxons gave to the *'place by the old straight (Roman) road'*.

**Runtlings** is Anglo-Saxon for *'stubble meadow'* . . .

. . . while nearby **Chickenley** was the *'chicken meadow'* (by the way, there was a Horbury family called Chicken).

**Storrs Hill** was the *'stony hill'*, the sort of place where pigs might forage.

**Sowood** was Ossett's *'south wood'*.

**Gawthorpe** is Viking for *'Gauk's* (an ugly person's) *hamlet.'*

**Paleside** is Old English for *'place outside the palings of the deer park'.*

The Lord of the Manor of Wakefield's New Deer Park lay to the north of Ossett. In 1315 John, Clerk of Horbury, was fined sixpence for removing green wood from the Park. In 1631 Thomas Savile, the Lord of the Manor, wrote 'Upon Tuesdaie I entend to kill a Stagge in the Newe Park.' The park then contained about 220 fallow deer. Part of the boundary ditch is still visible north of Gawthorpe (OS grid ref. SE 274229).

# Town Hall

Built to a design by W. Hansock and Son between 1905 and 1908 on the site of the town's old Grammar School in the market place, the Town Hall is now famous for its Compton theatre organ, which is in effect a small orchestra operated by keyboard, stops and pedals. 'You have to be a combination of musician and plumber to play it!' said one enthusiast.

Ossett received its charter of incorporation from the Privy Council with a grand procession from the station to the town on August 16th 1890.

# Ossett Market

There were displays of bull-baiting in the market place until 1811. The old *Cock and Bottle* Inn nearby had a reputation for cockfighting until the 1850s. Ossett Feast was held during Trinity Week and in September it was usual for the young men of Ossett to turn up in force at the Alverthorpe Feast for a running battle with the locals.

A letter of 1852 tells us that in Ossett flour was 1s. 8d. per stone, sugar 2½d.-6d. per lb., a leg of mutton 6d. and beef 3½d.-6d. per lb. More bargains; in 1789 an Ossett cloth maker, John Chappell agreed to sell his wife Barbery (along with all her clothing), to John Harford, weaver of Netherton, for three guineas.

Lee Gap Fair, Britain's oldest surviving horse-fair, had it's origins in Viking times. King Stephen granted it a charter in 1136. It is currently held at West Ardsley, 2 miles north of Ossett.

### The war memorial

(1928) commemorates the 230 Ossett men killed in the 1914-18 war. The bronze figure, cast by Walkers of Idle, is from a sculpture by R.L.Clark. **The 'Peace' plaque** of 1814 is from a Church of England Sunday School which stood nearby.

# Library

The library, designed by W.A.Kendall, was originally the Mechanics Institute and Technical School which opened in 1890 with 119 students and 18 staff. It also housed the town's Magistrate Court. The Court's first case in 1894 was that of a soldier charged with being drunk and disorderly. He was presented with a suit, a pair of boots and a good dinner and sent on his way to Halifax!

The borough took over the building in 1897 to celebrate Victoria's Diamond Jubilee.

# Yorkshire Bank

From 1894 to 1900, when the Yorkshire Penny Bank opened it's branch here, this was the premises of Ossett sub-postmaster and chemist J. W. Cussons. His initials can still be seen in a decorative carving on the Prospect Road wall of the building which was designed by W.A. Kendall. Cussons left Ossett to become a manufacturing chemist making Imperial Leather soap.

# Temperance Hall

Now called Saga House, the Temperance Hall was built in 'seventeenth century style modernised' to a design by Ossett architect W.A.Kendall in 1888. The new borough council met here until the Town Hall opened in 1908. The first Mayor was Edward Clay, a rag and mungo merchant. E. Clay & Son still have premises on Wesley Street.

The manufacture of mungo and shoddy, textiles made from woollen rags, helped put Ossett back on its feet after a severe slump.

# Barclays' Bank

The former Wakefield and Barnsley Union Bank was built in 1870 by Eastwood and Tolson of Ossett to an Italian Renaissance design by architect William Watson of Barstow Square, Wakefield. 'All timber to be of best red Baltic produce,' Watson insisted, 'clear of sap, shakes, large or loose knots, wavy edges or other defects.' Elland sandstone was used in the walling with a roof of Bangor countess slate. (Welsh slate was made available by the expanding railway network; Ossett had a station from 1865 until 1964. Flushdyke Station had opened in 1862). At least some of the carved heads on the keystones appear to be portraits.

In contrast to this little Venetian palace, 'Olly' Oakes sold tripe from a wooden hut next door.

The manager's house at the rear was equipped with nine bells, two gongs and a front door pull which cost 7/6d. After a merger with a Birmingham Bank in 1906 the bank amalgamated with Barclays in 1916.

# Pinfold

The pinfold on West Wells Road was where Ossett's Pinder impounded animals that strayed onto the town's three open fields; the North, the West and the Great or South field. There was a fine to be paid for the release of each animal (for example, a shilling for a cow and 4 pence for a sheep).

At the time of the Domesday survey, 1087, seven men using two ploughs tilled the fields of 'Osleset' which had a population of 25 to 30 people. The open fields were eventually enclosed following an inquiry which commenced in 1807.

# Mount Zion

In *Glimpses of Ossett's History* John Pollard lists ten churches and chapels built in the town between 1857 and 1867; 'an amazing outpouring of money and personal effort which was only possible because of the fervour of people's religious beliefs'. Mount Zion on Queen Street was built in 1863.

Methodism offered the 'solutions and answers that only religion can provide' to 'the hysteria and confusion of West Yorkshire people caught in social change' writes Glyn Hughes in *Millstone Grit*. He sees parallels between the charismatic travelling preachers with their 'colourful apocalyptic oratory' and today's rock stars. He compares the marginally differing Methodist groups with rock-music cults.

Ossett had it's own sect, the Inghamites led by Benjamin Ingham (*b.*1712, a distant relative of his namesake on *p.20*), who preached with his friends the Wesley brothers whom he met as a student at Oxford.

# Holy Trinity

In 1861 Benjamin Ingham, a member of an old Ossett family, then British Consul in Sicily, put forward the idea of building this landmark of a parish church on the town's newly acquired burial ground, offering £1,000 towards the project. Designed in Gothic style by ecclesiastical architect William Henry Crossland, it was completed in 1865 when a peel of bells, cast by Taylor's of Loughborough, was brought from Flushdyke Station in a procession led by a brass band.

Ossett's church had been a chapel-of-ease for Dewsbury Parish Church from 1409 until 1858. A former Holy Trinity church had been built in the market place in 1806 in classical style, partly at the expense of the perpetual curate, the Revd. Edward Kilvington (1767-1835), a man who became so stout that the Sexton hauled him into the specially designed three-decker pulpit using a primitive chair-lift.

In 1846 South Ossett, which then had about
700 inhabitants, became a parish in its own
right, although Ossett-cum-Gawthorpe
remained part of the Dewsbury parish until
1858. Christ Church was built in 1851.

# Christ Church, South Ossett

Richard Bell
1983

There were 1,900 burials here between 1851 and 1889 when further burials were allowed in the Wesleyan Burial Ground. In 1890 a South Ossett man was buried, according to his express wishes, upright so that he would be able to spring to his feet on the day of Resurrection.

In 1853 a vicarage was built next to the church. It's commanding view across the valley was later blocked by two large houses built by two men who'd had a difference with the first Vicar. They both later failed in business! *(the Parish magazine suggests that there's a moral to be learnt here!)*

23

# Brockson Carpets

The 'rapid growth in the district, especially South Ossett, is really marvellous,' reported *Wakefield Express* in August 1861, 'Buildings are springing up on all sides, the demand for houses being great. Near to Giggal Hill *(west of Manor Road crossroads)* a considerable number of workmen are engaged in the erection of 40 substantial cottage houses.'

The second branch of the Ossett Co-operative Society opened in 1871, ten years after the Society was founded. 'The lively little clock-tower of the brick and stone Manor Road branch,' is described by Kate Taylor in *Wakefield Heritage* as 'only less of a landmark than, say, the spire of the Parish Church, or the vast tank of Gawthorpe water tower.' By 1895 the Society was trading in coal, footwear, drapery, dressmaking, millinery and furnishings as well as groceries. The 2,070 members of the Society received a 'divvy of 3/6d in the pound. In contrast 1922 was described as 'the most trying year' with the smallest profit (£5,900) since 1884 and the staff put on short time.

# Park House

Now the home of Ossett School, Park House on Storrs Hill Road was built in sumptuous Victorian Gothic style in the 1860s or 70s for the Ellis family, mill owners, who are said to have made their fortune supplying uniforms to both sides during the Franco-Prussian war.

They owned the adjacent Victoria Mills (now Burmatex). A big slump hit the weaving trade in 1880 forcing the family to put the house up for sale. For a while it was used for the convalescence of victims of a smallpox epidemic (the isolation hospital was nearby in the 1894 brick terrace on Storrs Hill). Ossett Corporation purchased Park House for £2,500

and the Grammar School with its 95 pupils and 7 staff moved in on 24th September 1906.

Boy and girl pupils acted as volunteer fire-watchers during World War II, sleeping the night in an attic room at Park House ready to go on patrol when the warning sirens sounded. In the days of rationing a group of the older pupils went, with staff, to stay at Spalding High School* for a month's potato picking.

* and, latterly, to Bishop Burton, E.R. of Yorkshire

# Goring House

The slightly sulphureous spring waters of
Ossett Baths were said in 1829 to be
'celebrated for curing the gout, rheumatism
and the scrofula'. The Spring End
Cheltenham Baths nearby offered 'medicated
vapour, sulphureous, sitting, shower and
plunge baths'.

As part of a plan to turn the spa into 'a
second Harrogate' the tightrope walker
Blondin (1824-97) performed at the spa's
Montpelier Pleasure Grounds in Easter

1884. Avenues laid out and planted with limes remain but promoters of the scheme went bankrupt. A Mr Tennant, who is thought to have built Goring House as a kind of show house for the scheme, is said to have committed suicide there.

From 1961 until 1988 Goring House was the home of novelist Stan Barstow.

---

**The Tram depot** at the end of Sowood Lane is

now a Highway Materials Testing Laboratory. The line ran via Wakefield to the Belle Isle depot in Agbrigg. The first trams ran on 14th August 1904, the last, the no. 60, to Agbrigg on 24th July 1932. The Yorkshire (West Riding) Electric Tramways Co. ran all routes on this side of Ossett from 1911. Dewsbury & Ossett Tramways had their depot on Church Street (still extant almost opposite Woodheads').

# Gawthorpe Water Tower

On November 6th, 1910, a vast inrush of water flooded the workings of Pildacre Colliery at a rate of 30,000 – 50,000 gallons an hour. One man who saw it said the pumps, which were working at full pressure, might as well have been standing for all the impression they were making. 250 men and boys found themselves out of work.

Pildacre waterworks (now demolished) was opened on February 25th, 1928. Two pumping engines, named Maud and Edith by the Mayoress of Ossett, pumped water from the shaft and up to the water tower at Gawthorpe one and a quarter miles away.

The tower's concrete tank is 25 feet deep and holds 200,000 gallons. The Pildacre water supply was used until 1974 when Ossett's increasing area of housing, paving and roads began to seal off the supply of rainwater to the aquifer.

1983

# Low Laithes

Oliver Cromwell is said to have stayed the night here. The house was built around 1550 using a framework of oak beams held together by oak pegs. The frame was prefabricated, with marks carved on the main beams to aid assembly on site. The walls were a lattice of studs and pieces of split oak on which plaster was applied.

The original farmhouse became the centre of an H-block as wings, containing barns and extra living accommodation were added over the next 200 years. This gave protection to the central farmhouse, which was also given an 18 inch thick cladding of brick on its north side. Much of the original H-block has now been demolished.

Low Laithes Golf Club opened in 1925 as a nine hole course.

**The Red Lion** sits by the Dewsbury Road, once part of the Wakefield-Halifax turnpike, approved by Act of Parliament in 1740, for parts of which Blind Jack of Knaresborough (1717-1810) was the surveyor. The last toll bars at Ossett and Dewsbury were removed on 14th May 1866. This stretch follows the line of a Roman road that passed through Streetside.

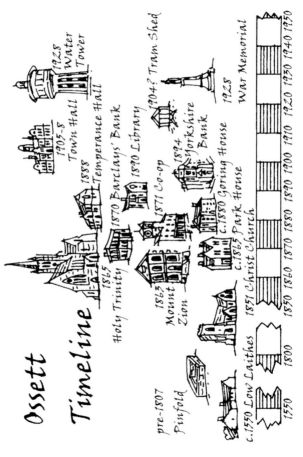

Ossett

Timeline

pre-1807 Pinfold

c.1550 Low Laithes

1857 Christ Church

1863 Mount Zion

1865 Holy Trinity

c.1865 Park House

c.1880 Goring House

1870 Barclays' Bank

1871 Co-op

1890 Library

1888 Temperance Hall

1894 Yorkshire Bank

1905-8 Town Hall

1928 Water Tower

1904? Tram Shed

1928 War Memorial

1550  1800  1850  1860  1870  1880  1890  1900  1910  1920  1930  1940  1950

River Don

Ossettia

Black Sea

# And finally...

Near the Black Sea there is an area called Ossettia.

Today's 700,000 North and South Ossettians are herdsmen and horsemen, probably descended from the Scythian warrior nomads of ancient Greek times.

Like the first settlers of Yorkshire they use the word 'Don' for river and, like the people of Ossett, they chose the fleece as an emblem. A fleece being fashioned into a garment is shown on a Scythian chief's gold regalia.

Scythia

Ossett 1906

Is there a connection? Greek legend tells us that Jason and the Argonauts took the Golden Fleece by river journey from the Black Sea to the North Sea – a route well known to the Vikings who are thought to have founded Ossett.

Ossett

River Don

North Sea

**My thanks to;**
Neville Ashby, Connie Barstow, Steve Chapman, Janet Nash, Dorothy Wainwright and, especially, to Ruth Nettleton.

**Publications consulted;**
Ossett and District Historical Society;
*Cockburn's Ossett* (1987)
*Ossett Inner Town Trail* (1984)
Rev. H.R.Haworth, *History of Christ Church* (1960?)
John Pollard, *Glimpses of Ossett's History* (1983)
Kate Taylor, *Wakefield District Heritage* (1976)

*Dragon's head, Town Hall, 1905-8*

*Fleeces at Nettletons & Porters, fellmongers, Ossett 1998.*

For more about Ossettia see *Searching for the Scythians*, National Geographic, September 1996

**Illustrations** by the author.